SKETCHES FOR A BOOK OF PSALMS

SKETCHES FOR A BOOK OF PSALMS

Ira F. Stone

1/30/02

For Judith

I have enjoyed our learning together. Thank you for your enthusiasm and insight

STON

Library of Congress Number: 00-191132
ISBN #: Softcover 0-7388-2324-4

To order additional copies of this book, contact:
Xlibris Corporation
1-888-7-XLIBRIS
www.Xlibris.com
Orders@Xlibris.com

CONTENTS

BEFOREWORD

The need to cry out is insatiable and unmediated by reason or experience. We cry out despite the quality of the response to our cry. In fact, the silence goads our crying and crying. Cries of pain; cries of joy; cries of wonderment and betrayal; we cannot live without them. Despite all, we do live. When it makes no sense or we'd rather not; miracle and curse, we live. Crying makes us human.

Should we be guilty for that? There are days when the sheer magnitude of the violence and madness of life and the inability of anything, least of all poetry, to vitiate that madness and violence, threaten to render even one who has escaped the power of night silent. I live therefore I cry. I cry with the silence of those who do not live, offering it up to its source: the silence to whom we cry. To the silence beforeword whose word we must be, we must be. We have no choice. We are commanded, compelled, without explanation, to be, to live, to cry out.

Pray, Lord,
pray to us
we are near

"Tenebrae"
Paul Celan

Our God cometh and doth not keep silence

Psalm 50 V.3

No man can by any means redeem his brother
Nor give God a ransom for him —
Far too costly is the redemption of their soul
and must be let alone forever

Psalm 49 V. 8

Words change shape and come to have
other meanings in other languages.
How do we know the unspoken stays the same?

"Speeches"
William Bronk

BOOK ONE

Psalm I

Hold something

For as long as the muscles
my fingers
keep gripping

Longer

As long as the clock face
across the square
even without hands
holds on
goes on showing
the possibility of time

Something of you
to last   Longer
than the flowers I could praise
or children

Something complete

All light or all dark

Unadulterated unchanging
unutterable   Desire

Psalm II

The night gives way
to a clarifying downpour

Altar fires are impossible

There will be no sacrifices

Thanksgiving offerings
now stranded
eternally suspended
stretching

We grow older racing
to keep up with them
but not unconditionally

Sequestered fire memories
disguised in words
in a caress on
these dark mornings
offering the day
its glory

Its glory
like the skittering
starlings across
the slick surfaces

Psalm III

...robbed...voiceless
ache   aching
song aches
uncovers
a suspicion
of comfort
pinions
shadow
shelter
toward healing
suffices forever

Psalm IV

As if cleansed

A faint mix
of melody

call it new

If I can lift
the heart's
disbelief
the shoulder's
growing stoop

There may be
no more than
a single clear
shower of snow
to break the
last warmth
or as surprise
in the turning
anticipation of
imminent rebirth

Then as if
cleansed of the
future

on a faint mix
of melody

call it new

song

Psalm V

Which voice
sculpting
word-in-formation
of the heart or
those engraved
in the air pursuing
mercy

Rebuked

Chastised

In the end
a simple prayer
not for the dead

withhold anger

Psalm VI

Morning is
surprise
repeated

Like the probability
of angels
in chorus

Psalm VII

Timelessness
bumps into memory

Time folds in on
timelessness
pricked by what
refuses
homogeneity

Martyrdom

The death of a child

My child

Instances of lovemaking

Recriminations

Love again

When

Psalm VIII

a psalm
a song for the Sabbath Day

Waters
swirl
destabilize
drown
divide
nourish
soothe
cleanse
uproot
evaporate
return
quench
carry
are absorbed
expelled
might be
mistaken
for all

A tree and a man
root themselves
withal

Psalm IX

Journeys
interminable
depths again
deeper depths
deeper
depths again
deeper
still
without bottom
is eternity
over which
is Lord
forever
who reigns
rules
Those are
the rules
are Lord

Psalm X

Sing the curvature
of questions
and dance
mountains
at the embrace
of lovers
brides and grooms
along its
lengthening
spine
Without their
music
follows
the dense
point
we place
below
and stops

Psalm XI

a psalm;
a song for the dedication of a house

Out of the earth
shape takes shape
and takes whatever
spirits buried there
believed themselves
at home
We build homes
displacing ourselves
into the space
reserved but too
dark too moist
We lift ourselves
by structure from
the pit our tears
transformed to mortar
our sins to brick

Psalm XII

Thickets
thorns
blood
bleeding
scabbing
healing

Heals
inevitably
invisibly
darkly

Promises
and
delivers

Swiftly
finished
cut-off
and grows
and keeps on
growing

Psalm XIII

Encamped
outside
the city

Drawn
outside by
promises

Always outside
where justice
decamps

Outside
refuge
where justice
belongs

Outside
longing
with the
advance of
pilgrims
who return
year
by
year

Outside
weeping

Psalm XIV

At the last hour
before dawn
trepidation
hesitation

The hills hold
their breath

In mid-step
mountains
hover
darkening
space

Sometime
it stays that way
for ages
generations
without sky

But it is there

Sometime

Dawn

Praise

Psalm XV

No eagles...
We search the sky—
to bear us
to shelter
But the search
the expanse
presents itself
a glory distant
within which we
yet move hardly
discerning where
it begins—
it doesn't—
nor ends
Do we
No more
nor less
and in this
glory we live
more calm

Psalm XVI

Carry
the wilderness

How it still
feeds

How the fear
of it passes

How its weight
learns to lift
us to its lips
and give suck

How we wander
intimately
in its arms
until movement
is illusion
and we are
rested

Psalm XVII

A psalm for the first day of the week

In the weaving
of sunlight and
sadness — the shadows
of stories broken-off
beginning again
full breathed
arbitrary but
restored
Resuming a meandering
as if down followed
up and after
followed before
As if hope followed
birth and birth
repeats itself in
measured units of
the Sun's movements

Psalm XVIII

The world bends
toward evening
eyes lifted
straining out
at the edge
where light
and black
Turns back peering
into its own eye
Thankfully always
peering back
despite us

Psalm XIX

Praise the outside
of ourselves
Where it touches
the returning sun
after a rocky honeymoon
when the black skies
complete their secret
accompaniment

Praise the fear
that we will disappear
We will

Praise the outside
that only disappears
in small measures

We tremble but cannot
count its comings and goings

Live in praise
fleetingly

Psalm XX

Of Thanksgiving

Almost visible
the outline
of a specter
lifting—we can
name it terror–

Behind
what's left exposed
revels and trembles
in its exposure
coming as close
as we know
to thanksgiving for
a distant possibility
of safety

Prayer for protection
without hardness

Wary of pain
we endure
this moment's
pleasure

Psalm XXI

a psalm of forgetting

Savage
without hope
wordless
when it all comes back

We pray
then
that it doesn't

We pray to forget
that we may pray

Psalm XXII

Imagine
emptiness
strewn with
words
by which we
are consigned
darkly
all too daily
and if you
dare regard
the deeds that
brought us
Desire us back
We will return
We haven't really
gone anywhere and
there's nowhere
else to go

Psalm XXIII

Shadow is permanent
resistant
unfazed by names
Rock
Shepherd

Yes
there are depths

Yes
I call
as though led a
complicated route

Still waters

Sheep overflow

My cup
My enemies

The house
for long days

Psalm XXIV

Creates
the eye
sees or
hears or desires
sight or sensible
sound

We arrange
sensations
making laws
of them

Who
sees the contours
or defines
justice

Still we learn
love
from it
when we're
able

Psalm XXV

A Psalm
A Song of the Infinitesimal

Praise –
The star
exploded
over
ancient
ancestors
Its light
reaches us
just now
indifferent to
the length of
its demise
Whether we see it
or they saw it
or not
It will fade
longer than
the span of
our story
Equally indifferent
a star perhaps
explodes now
its fading light
the future

Psalm XXVI

A Pilgrim song

But any home
we could have
had
is death
Sometimes
we pretend
otherwise
Pick up
your stick
now
pilgrim
Sing

Psalm XXVII

Silence
A Psalm of Praise

Inside
where words
engage the
purity
of song
unspoiled
by voice
they don't exist

But struck by a passing
intuition that they must
come from somewhere
some real place
we sing them with
their silence intact

Psalm XXVIII

A Song For the House
A Psalm of Zion

Defeat is vast

But we call You
land
city
house
that we may
breathe

leaving the
emptiness
hidden at the
center hidden

We tremble
at the blood
it costs

Bewildered
we spend

Psalm XXIX

A Song For the House
A Psalm of Zion

Rebuilding
as always
as if rebuilding
Your house
we would be

It never lasts
it can't
neither can we
nor You
Only both

Psalm XXX

A Pilgrim Song

Strain...
the road's discomfort—
in the air longing
for home
They come—
I come—
unable to rest
in any city
in any embrace
The anxiety—
the relief
always ahead
of the music
(I awake) mixing
with the trail
dust in my
nostrils
vowing to stop
but unfaithful
reconnoiter peace

Psalm XXXI

On what instrument
Strings tied
Bundling bodies
For burial
Unaccompaniable

Prophets speechless

As though no air
carries sound

Not as though
although distant
never removed

It is with us
With You
Is it

Pray with what breath
left

Interrupt
or not
It is past time

Even today
Worse — banal

There is something
to weep

(cont)

Weep
or not
It is past time
It is maddening
to call

Can't

Then what
What is the fate
of questions

Psalm XXXII

With no preliminaries

A word from the glint
of sun striking words
in our hands they've
traveled far they've
seen more truth than
blood more certainty
than faith — can you
make them out

You sing them again
we'll listen we'll write
we'll copy we'll compose
we'll translate you
make the shofar
stop the knives

Not even the knives
anymore but the ever
raised arm whether
it falls or not
the futile ram's blood

You sing
We'll listen
Bless us
Re-Name us
Hallelujah

Psalm XXXIII

A Psalm of Solace

Waves
rise
wordlessly

A
breeze

Summer
persists

Psalm XXXIV

A Psalm of Listening

In your beginning

We listen
for The Good

lifesound/deathsound

so brief
eternally

it is in this
Good

We listen
learn to listen

One day

Psalm XXXV

Broken themes recur
in broken segments

single words that
escape the conflagration

refugees of a world
behind the world

Outside

is such a word
comes to us from
the fire beyond the fire

Waiting for it
day after day
beginning with
its arrival

Sent to us

A recursive
prayer

It divides
and is our only
reconciliation

Psalm XXXVI

Lightburdened...
Sourceless...
Sometimes bending
in submission
to no avail
Or standing tall
in the circle of
light also to no
avail the burden
unaffected as its
source...prayers
finding their own
words in the
perplexity
That burden
too

Psalm XXXVII

The trumpet face
lifts
lags
mutes
scats
swings
over the neck of the
sax
the stroll of the
piano
and the keepers
of your gates
your city
jump or
linger
in ballad
Hear it all...
Singing with your voice

Psalm XXXVIII

Gardens crest
along the walls
bursting color
in the cracks
even occasionally
reviving

Psalm XXXIX

A Repentance Song

Distant light
invites
voice
turned
into song
heard —
saving
and at the end
safe

Psalm XL

A Psalm of Correspondence

Addressed –
the tangle
of words
tumbled out
at the core
shaped our bodies
Re-strung the
harps of memory
the suites of
compassion –
Our hearing
you hearing us
Listen is your word
we have made ours –
Listen

Psalm XLI

The snows of sorrow
bury too many –
called
Avramka
Feiga
Basha
Hinda
Fishel
Sora
Chenya
Anshel
Shamot
Hamiforash
Divine
Names
parsed
plowed
parched
pleaded
bled
sown
seedling
standing
names
calling
instead
now
eternal

BOOK TWO

Psalm XLII

No cries in the air
ghosts
hover alive
denied
This second death
preceding a first
and now a third
no cries in the air

The still air –
sunscarred –
closing in on us all

White noise of suffering
batters its exquisite
silence over and over
against your sky

An amusement park
world tiring of
motion altogether
limps by the waters
of your conquered
sea amid your monsters'
broken body parts

No cries in the
unfathomable air

Psalm XLIII

In our celebrations
of time your
eternity as wilderness
feeds us unbid
undeserved
ungrateful
Then in the night
words remember
their definitions
dancing their way
homeward for a
day or dislocated
two

Psalm XLIV

Voices
in a forest
of bone
rise into
an altar
of their own

Crossing skies...
Bridegroom
chariot
Light
blocked
blackened
visible
cunning
comforting
by turns

Stacked
the waiting
carcasses
for a sweet
savor

jammed
backed-up
stuck
longing
satisfaction

(cont)

Voices
in a forest
of bone
rise into
an altar
of their own

Psalm XLV

A Psalm of Secrets

Into the grove
of enemies
drawn
grasped
surrounded

Enemies...enemies
Are there not
enough
or endless

What of olives
and figs and

children's
children

A grove
of words
torn
pages
flutter in
the aimless
wind

madness
piety

Psalm XLVI

morning
call
breaks

Storms

then
cool
memory
clears

selecting
mercy

Psalm XLVII

Wait
wait
wait
wait
wait
wait

See
see
see
see
see
see

Answer
answer
answer
answer
answer
answer

Forever
forever
forever
forever
forever
forever

Psalm XLVIII

The wing of cherubim
closer
nearly
sacrificed
our multiple
faces
They are our eyes
looking
from you
to us
seeing double
or nothing

Psalm XLIX

A Pilgrim Psalm

Cracked toes
of mortality
angels with bones
and frail hearts —
with rage
with jealousy
lower...

Angel's soles
define our upper
limits not high
enough to view
the world except
in its pieces
Lift us...

We walk...

Psalm L

For the Leader
A Song

Toppled
tainted
detached
demystified

troops
riches
power...

stained
disbelieved
lavished
praised

indifferently

To whom

Psalm LI

For the Leader

Out of shoes
we call
from suitcases
we sing
across
bomb sites
which lay
buried over
burial sites
we follow
but it is late
and we are
learning to
forget

Psalm LII

For the Leader

imageless
Elohim
b'zelem b'panim
el panim
blank
beyond
recognition
we do not
recognize
one another
that is our
faith — that
we are
recognizable
that is the
image
ha-demut shelacha
m'demut
l'demamah

Psalm LIII

For the face of the Leader

Veiled
we turn away
from the face
turned us
away veiled
this way and
that way
despite its
indistinctness
We look
We will
always look
For we have
eyes
See

Psalm LIV

שקט
שקד
שקר
שכר
שחר

על ההרים
עצי שקדים
eyes on
the morning
mountains
drunk
with hope
where the black
begins to break
barely breathing
נשמת כל חי
לעת לעת

Psalm LV

For the dancers
A Psalm

Moon rises with
lifting
legs — light
brokered from
something past
and not yet come
But the flesh
of it the sinews
their contorted
tradition light
and loosed a
song of joy

Psalm LVI

A Psalm Of Love

Dawnmists
embrace
before speech
the embrace
of dawn
mists
and chanted
voicelessly
A wonder

Psalm LVII

A Psalm Of Love

Shades turn
shadow souls
star children
sands sleep
peacefully
removed from
the pounding
sea dazzled

Psalm LVIII

A Psalm Of Love

Deserts midday
Caves ringed
the accretion
of martyrs
offering shade
spring
fed wells
opened closed
opened contended
Sustaining

Psalm LIX

A Psalm Of Love

After mists
of day heat
burn away
leaving exposed...

Thus able to soar
as though —

Soaring and
simultaneously
sheltered

TON

Psalm LX

A Psalm Of Love

In the midnight
of embrace the
flesh parts
The folds of
voices imprinting
the scroll of
former sorrows
eternal erasure-bliss

Psalm LXI

A Psalm Of Love

Autumn
of reminiscence
A blinding morning
sun so unexpected
Breezes wrap
around the air
between us
As though you
passed by us
suddenly remembered

Psalm LXII

A Psalm Of Love

Buoyed by
a reprieve
however
temporary
the inevitably
moribund
lovers — mother
separating
from her child —
soldiers —
slaves
Staring back
inexplicably
peaceful
Never-the-less

Psalm LXIII

A Psalm Of Love

Harrowing moon
hugely half-eaten
hung in the
shortening sky
traveling toward
ice darkness
We punctuate
your demise with
animal howls
with horns

Psalm LXIV

A Psalm Of Love

Harvesting poisons
infiltrate what
remains from the
picked fields and
feed the eruption
of new forms
new life
Maggots and
worms giving
thanks before
the freeze to
life and to what
sustains life undaunted

Psalm LXV

A Psalm Of Love

Never silent
beneath layer
upon layer

stillness...

hibernation

the promise
of warmth

the buried odor
of remembered

touch among
a chorus of

black angels
impassioned but
never silent

-STON

Psalm LXVI

A Psalm Of Reconciliation

Not easy
הנר יהוה
from heights
firmaments
gone soft
נשמת אדם
a torch
swaying in
a salt lick
חיות השדה
shelter
trembling
trembling

Psalm LXVII

A Psalm Of Reconciliation

gathered from stone
cold
pressed
earthen
patched
emptied
light
in its terror
seeks seeing

Psalm LXVIII

A Psalm Of Reconciliation

Stones
sky fallen
stacked
ladderly
twin-poled
in a crag
moonlight
returns
invites
ascension

Psalm LXIX

False
songs
midnight
lips
call
hearts
betrayed
betrayed
sing
desperate
choice
you listen
listen
you
midnight
blankets
blank
its
song
soothes

-STON

Psalm LXX

A Psalm Of Reconciliation

Stunned
earth
flood
remnant
drunk
degraded
as in a
dream
Rising
clouds
amid
thunder
blindness
binds
us
bound
and bound

Psalm LXXI

A Psalm Of Reconciliation

Breath held
sunset
does not flinch

A birthcry
the skinslit
of memory

Score years
more years
years at all

Calibrated
in wilderness

betrothed
and
rescued

Psalm LXXII

תהילה של שלמה

בלב השמים
אין אבל טפת
אור
ראינו
מהגילוי הנסתרה
הכל מלא
הכל קול
מעבר המדבר
לפחות
יש זאות

BOOK THREE

-STON

Psalm LXXIII

A Psalm of Abraham

Blood moment
measured and
sand blotted
fine grained
leather stropped
stopped and
stooped bereft
left less
than a corpse

Psalm LXXIV

A Psalm of Sarah

Broken joy
ordinary
picture
We grow
we give
life fattens
until all
vanity is
wind on
the small
hills that
slowly enlarge
and take our
breath...

Psalm LXXV

A Psalm of Isaac

Never sunrise —
never
dawn

Psalm LXXVI

A Psalm of Rebecca

Knotted birth blood
in love with God's
ghost — mother
daughter sister
wife refugee of
a hunter's boots

We all spin oracles
of sadness lived
more torn in our
inevitable knowledge
but doing what we can
to collaborate

Psalm LXXVII

A Psalm of Hagar

Thirst
is endless
the cliffs...
infants
thirst
endlessly
the sky
wells
the war
wells
the home
wells
a furtive
drink
forgotten

Psalm LXXVIII

A Psalm of Ishmael

Screaming
muscles
will not
scream
silently

Psalm LXXIX

A Psalm of Jacob

Night
tents
old
wounds
names
nothing
repairs
among
strangers

Psalm LXXX

A Psalm of Rachel

Mothersleep
along the
roadside
under your
pillar of
stones
quarried
agelessly
in transit
neither
home
nor exiled
mothersleep
orphanmother
without
speech
stolen
mother

Psalm LXXXI

תהלה פ'א

תהלת לאה

על המזבח של פרחים
רכות עניים כדי לא לראות
את הידיד בפיו הזריד האפילה
את האש העלה על המזבח הפרחים --
חן חן ביחד
לא לראות

Psalm LXXXII

A Psalm of Esau

Wordtangle —
skin and wives
in the wild
country of red
red loyalty
red love
red abandonment —
wild red
sunsets
sunrise
bracket
night loss
night lost
in a kiss

Psalm LXXXIII

A Psalm of Joseph

Scorpions
waterless
pits

we hoard
and build
dress like
everyone else

But nothing
wrests
a blessing
from the wrong
son's head

STON

Psalm LXXXIV

A Psalm of Israel

Neverhealed
cavetaken
boneborne
hoaryheaded
flightroads
directionwild
offeredashes
snatchedangels
plaguewarning
innocence
and
retribution

Psalm LXXXV

A Psalm of the Daughters of Dinah

Death disfigured
by their blood
They die without
death with my shout
in their nostrils eternally

Psalm LXXXVI

A Psalm of Moses the man of God

Manfire
unconsumed
the smoke
dwells

Psalm LXXXVII

A Psalm of Aaron

Disfigured
spreadfingers
lambsblood
always the
gold
extracted

Psalm LXXXVIII

A Psalm of Korach

Outside the circle
a mass grave
never overflows

Psalm LXXXIX

תהלה פ'ט

תהילת דוד

אשרי פניך
על הגדר
בין כתר
לתפילה
יותר טוב
מהדברים
רעבים
עד סוף
השמים
העתיד

TON

BOOK FOUR

Psalm XC

A Psalm of Turning

No warmth
pirouetting sun
frosts in summer
butterflies
ice spinning
the spider's
ice web
not the
tingle of
melting
except in
a word
melody
caught on
their lips
your breath
stuck in
their throats
and we
attend

Psalm XCI

A Psalm of Persisting

Under cover of moss
bonedust
nurtures
broken roots
into a twisted
tree
sterile
sacred
pockbarked
in a sandy
loam
rising
reluctantly
youward

Psalm XCII

A Refugee Psalm

Black teeth
in the mirror
where the others
see white
In the heart
they are black
teeth blinking
garbage eater
to the others
who are not
our mothers
who will not
answer prayers
Who
will not
answer

Psalm XCIII

A Psalm Of Immigrants

Our sad mouths
filled with song
and all came
out wrong

Psalm XCIV

A Pilgrim Song

Only eyes
remain at
the end of
the journeys

Lift our eyes

We chant
lift our eyes

or soften
their seeing

into song

Psalm XCV

A Pilgrim Song Of Survival

Crossing borders
dawnlight
twilight
lightspeckled
lightbearing
gravelighting
lifelighting
wordlighting
lightlighting
lightsinging

Psalm XCVI

A Psalm A Confession

Nightjudging
afflicted souls
numberless
remain suspended
in affliction
Enumerating
One blood
Two blood
One interval
between blood
Two intervals
between blood
We bleedconfess
We bleed

Psalm XCVII

A Psalm of separation

Splitsea covered words
muffle direction…

spin-off below surfaces
float as bait to gulls
swooping…

Carrion lifted —

Psalm XCVIII

A Psalm of separation

Embedded
love
light
solace...
The living
are miners
who mine
until
blood

And the dead
are dead
beyond digging

Psalm XCIX

A Psalm of separation

Wordwalls
desertbarbed
doubletongued
memoryleaded
and bookbound
call
chantmuscles
raising dust
to hide behind
you
in the chippedwalldust
holding

Psalm C

A Psalm of separation

Glassair
smokesoaked
the music
arrested
impeded
returned
insubstance
to
insubstance

Psalm CI

Hymnwhispers
waiting
echoremnants
of the deaf
barely calling
banishedwords
back into a
language semblance
breathing א

Psalm CII

A Psalm of Separation

Instinct decays
proficiently
borne on absent wings —
only air disturbed
in a passed
mass flutter
voiced

Psalm CIII

A Psalm of separation

Lingered
edges
of festive
boughs
bathed
burnt
brandished

Offerings
poured
spilled
soaked
marrowed

bloodbound
joy
parting

Psalm CIV

A Psalm of separation

Everlonging
glance
behind —
an angel's
perspective —
strewn petals
of sodden
history —
Light is
evermorning...
Compassion
blinds our eye

Psalm CV

A Psalm of separation

Bridgebroken
we stare over
landscrapped
emptylanded
gerriedgeography
Sunken stories
strung islands
between us
a measure
of distance
your hand
measures
sand slipping
between washed
away and
still drying

Psalm CVI

תהלה ק'ו

תהלת הפרישה

שוב
ושוב
הענן
עלה
ואין
בה
מה

נשם
מעולם
לא הגיע

עדיין
הגדיל
ההרים
להבדיל
בין לילה
לעוד לילה

BOOK FIVE

STON

ALEPH

Psalm CVII

Hidden
stones
lace
beneath
the toil
of scripture
freightbearing
backcracking
crawlbacking

(cont)

BET

caringforward
promising
Wanders
idolatrously
and
idolatrously

(cont)

GIMMEL

bonded
with all
futurebearing
songbreaths
worldbreathing
Kingly
dispersed
discussing
onesided
dialogue
praying
in questions

(cont)

DALET

questions
from song
breath
from breath
breathes deeply
lungflame
Hollowsocketed
staunching
wordbearing
more
no
words
But across rivers

(cont)

HAY

conquests
desertblooming
survivalmiracle
breathing
back
songpraise
ashflower
songs of
tomorrow's

praise
tomorrow

Psalm CVIII

A Stepping Up Song

Finally kissed by calm
Afternight wrestled
for remnantbreathed
we catch breath
ancient
glitterglyphs

lighten by
stark insistence
and the climb

Psalm CIX

A Stepping Up Song

Stammers in
twoorthreetongued
repetition and invention
Self illegible
untranslatable

comfortably foreign
filled to overflowing
but empty awaiting
to be filled

Psalm CX

A Stepping Up Song

From hills
mists
across
seas
carried on
smokewaves
dissipated
eastward
remembered

in every note
of every song
whistled a
bullet or bomb
marching

Psalm CXI

A Song of Deliverance

Mirrors
of flesh
that bloom
light at
all hours
undisturbed
by timecounting
Over blackrivers
droplets of

sustenance
drawn from
neverdead voices
They will not
be quieted

Psalm CXII

Heartvoiced
a labor
of mouthburned
speech escapes
a sigh a
meeting of shout
and faceless
enmity
A long ago
linger
of
land lover
of sightwracked
sky opening
of the most

dire brimstone
a still —
a frozen
dread
comes upon
u...s

Psalm CXIII

A Melody For Priests

Quite burial
the sun on
ruins goldens
and provides
visitors perspective
perpetrators
wear civilian clothes
explain the was

as is as will
never be as was
which wasn't's
Praise begin a
choir of praise
This after all
Praise

Psalm CXIV

A Melody of Praise

Hearts wordknitted
kissed in procession
laid out
blessed
read
returned
Return
resurrected
reresurrected

firefabric
skin
touched by
a bird's feather
flies
my soul
bless
you

Psalm CXV

Praiseyou
before sunrise
Praiseyou
darkness
implicit
of light
Praiseyou
in the chill

before winter
on the frozen
dew that melts
into yarzheit
that swims
into rivers
of unsurvivors
watering the world
with youpraise

Psalm CXVI

Ground stone
stormshifted
configures
coheres
as a cape
over the shoulders
of mercy mercy
long suffering name

until the thousandth
generation
regenerates
Until simply the
forever unfinished
yields an eternal
engine of hope
And praise wells
up explosively

Psalm CXVII

A Psalm at the Gate

Stragglers
on tattered
crowns

we take back
the seats
singing
Conjuring
first doves
of submission
then bows
of haunted
covenants

Psalm CXVIII

Showers of pure
dust
coarse
cleansing
damp sparks

of instruction
piece together
a familiar urn
aflame within
searching a myriad
of hands to order
the letters into laws
set out in the white
river succor of
another crossing

Psalm CXIX

Hands
that twist
the knot
of time

Lift them

Take and join
them to the
skyward canvas
of your imagetent

Touch them

Veil them
in the shadow
of your light

They are infinitely
raised

Restored

Psalm CXX

In the company
of worshippers

the sound of
solace
heartsound
grandfathersound
stalks rivers
of petition
ravines of
imploring
still sound
solace
in the end
evenstill

Psalm CXXI

A Stepping Up Song

At midnight the red sun
of memory is betrayed
by darkness doused
out of the sky of
childhood of captivity

The child the captive
released by blackening
images blinded into
a rejoicing of disappearing
released to imperceptibility

Blindly and gratefully
full grown and forgetful
limps and blathers
busily reinventing

forebears following forms

By morning after
the red sun has sworn
itself absent the notes
of a song a hymn
recur in angels' language
the chorus of visiting
gravemouths goad out
a song the vacant heavens
have heard have handed down

Psalm CXXII

A Stepping Up Song

Fatherweighted
along the route
of march
deaf making
circle our

song river
flows to
the fields
which welcome
us home
new home
barren beneath
the harvest
we celebrate
we sing new
praise fallowlipped

Psalm CXXIII

A Psalm of Redemption

Broken blooded
altar flesh
rising in tranquil
countryside
Not a breath
sustains the
lifedigging

diggers

But all talk
of blooded wounds
of night and
judgement still
sleeps in the
impeccable towers

What of lifewords
of bloodtithes
What of contrition

Psalm CXXIV

Bookboxed
all cries
echo echo
ineradicable
all cries
open

All cries open speech

speech
hold out
the chance
of meeting
all cries
are heard
by crying
all cries
are answered
No Matter
What

Psalm CXXV

Touched

fed
held
heard
seen
spoken to
received
washed
welcomed
worried over
raised
youpraised

Psalm CXXVI

Rising waters
drift into killing
rivers
burial flows
receiving
from of old
creationmud

transporting
to the sea
mighty breakers
thunderous
strength
broken pieces
voice and flamethrone
The blessing strength
The hewing voice
The sitting glory
The projected memory
The peace

Psalm CXXVII

A Psalm of Remembrance

Landlife
dug into
the wordlayers
unfolding on
the tongue —
the song of
planting
the muscle

memory of
harvest
full moons
and seven
circuited
celebrations
writing
grateful
light...
Engraving
on the thick
ever thicker
night sky

Psalm CXXVIII

Midnight music
bridges
between us

By healed-hearts
hollow-scarred
notes comfort
deepest suffering

For the others
there is sleep
and reawakening

Midnight
music follows
the expanding
curve

Wakeful

Psalm CXXIX

Someday
the harp
replays
its memory
of music
In darkness –
unheard –
hopepraises

Psalm CXXX

The worst of winters
disappear from all
but our remembering
Wind itself winding

to its song of spring's
forgetful new moon
New song
new moon
scattered
leaves pasted
to redrawn trees
now re-planted
staring down the
shadows
staring back

Psalm CXXXI

A Song for a New Time

Their past is past
for them but always
present for us
We crawl out
of the sea again
We sing you yet
another counting
another measure
beating

Psalm CXXXII

A Song for a New Time

After infinitely
One and one
again
always new
dated from today

one and again one
always new
Never before
again
Sevens
Tens
Yovels
Never now
always after
infinitely
starting
tomorrow
we'll expect
you

Psalm CXXXIII

A Song for a New Time

Newhearted
iceless
of facescape
unpocked
backgrounded
in smokeages
which never
disappear
but through
a dark wisdom
and without
the tyranny
of numbers
we measure

Psalm CXXXIV

A Song for a New Time

Mechanisms
techniques
gears
springs
pulleys
digital
softening
of the duration
of the obsession
to measure
New months
on charts
graphs

maps
grids
deciphering
the space
between
language
and
desire
splits
the clockhands
pulled by a
tideshower of
screams

Psalm CXXXV

A Song for a New Time

Such heavens that spin in bloodcircles
hallowed as a curse
Gave us those days a crust of bread
Left us dates on which to fend
for place names and families
on earth as it once was above
and spinning now only outward
reckless of your gifts
positioning our days as long as years
counting by lightspeed in contradiction of our
simple senses encountering a void a music and a memory
of speech writing itself right off of the page the skin but
as it is in such heavens

Psalm CXXXVI

A Psalm of Resurrection

No
body's
left
but
numb
rubbing
flesh --
organs...
recital...
limping
liturgies
עבודת
המקדש
flayed
offering bleeds
from one world to another
profusely enough to live
again forever dead

Psalm CXXXVII

A Psalm of Resurrection

Incomprehensible light
in an infant's eye
following the path
that one face takes
everywhere
anywhere
absolutely
or interrupted
by the sound
of a leaf
separating
from its branch
with melancholy
joy

Psalm CXXXVIII

A Psalm of Resurrection

Alignment of bone
burrowing
in humiliated search
for
parts
partners
classmates
not called
by song
yet song
the afflatus
of all birth
first birth
second birth
final birth
we sing
    implore

Psalm CXXXIX

A Psalm of Resurrection

Flowering open

mouths reaching
for songwords
for scourednotes
dropping from a
pastcloud as it
breaks up over
the painmountian
As it soothes itself
in snow — opens

to a blank page
ice hard
And they sing hard
flowering back
into the nature
of time
Returning to the very word
flower
lips
passion

Psalm CXL

A Psalm of Redemption

Night doesn't end
but lies hidden
in the dawnbreak
Be wary
לא תישן

Psalm CXLI

A Psalm of Redemption

Wordhidden
speech
is lighted
from within

Carries
over
the dread
timecalmed

childcalmed
everydayness
fixes a certain
innocent tantrum

on the face
wearied
forward

Psalm CXLII

A Psalm of Redemption

You met
embraced
fatigued
of song
of law
broken
of famine
now
we study
one another
Praise us
first
Return
we always
said
and we
will return
Your move
How will

we know
We know

Psalm CXLIII

A Psalm of Redemption

Candlespared
flame
selflighted
stillburning
deathlight/lifelight
fluctuating
shadow
childlike
wick
wavers
snuffed
blackens

the snuffer
fingers and
from its char
blazons

Psalm CXLIV

A Psalm of Redemption

Peacesplattered
whitememory
on black
parchment
quickened

unsacrificed
undismembered
in a joy rendered
rewording as though
youhear
youmatter
a heartmaking
word
a chastened kiss
still

Psalm CXLV

A Psalm of Praise
A Song of Joy

Counting backwards
from destiny
we sing
your fidelity
we are
your quillstrokes
your breath
we are

we sing

Psalm CXLVI

A Psalm of Praise
A Song of Joy

Ghostbanished
sun
moon
rivers
restored
flow
around
still
frozen
stones
down
to
a

retranquilled
sea
on its
shores
again
sand

Psalm CXLVII

A Psalm of Praise
A Song of Joy

Risenmist
snowmelt
softening
akin to
spring
Wildgrasses
groundcover
of dovefood
and nest
twigging
Sunsquint
damp but
striving
wakefully

Psalm CXLVIII

A Psalm of Praise
A Song of Joy

Praisenaming
facemaker
of forgetfulness

and lovespeaking
Fallen hammeretched
on the stillstone
heart of brokenblood
passing before the
humaneyed divine
finding voice
finding a nameworld
tumbling names out
praise giving
endless names
insufficient to
mute memory
praise giving
common name
written name
inerasible name
spoken out loud
name
life claiming
name
orgasmic
name
multiplying and
fruitful name
praise

Psalm CXLIX

A Psalm of Praise
A Song of Joy

Song calling
on the ever
hills the moved
mountain of
people flowing
back into blood
calling to one
another you
and you and
you there love
there work there
spell the letters
of our rescued
name there
our children there
our ever wary
fire there our
bellowing burn of
you praise remembered
and now named
Our name your name
world called
love called
called name praised
your name praised
יהוה

TRANSLATIONS

Psalm LII

line 2-God
line 3 - in the image in the face
line 4 - to face
line 17 - your image
line 18 - from image
line 19 - to silence

Psalm LIV

Silence
almond
lie
drunkenness
dawn (or darkness)

On the mountains
almond trees
eyes on
the morning
mountains
drunk
with hope
where the black
begins to break

barely breathing
the breath of all life
slowly

Psalm LXVI

line 2 - candle of God
line 6 - the soul of man
line 10 - beasts of the field

Psalm LXXII

A Psalm of Reconciliation
In the heart of the heavens
there is nothing but a drop
of light
we see
from the hidden revelation
all is full
all is voice
from beyond the wilderness
at least
there is this

Psalm LXXXI

A Psalm of Leah
On the altar of flowers
weak eyes in order not to see
the beloved in his mouth the
stalk of darkness

the fire that rises on the altar of
flowers —
grace grace together
not to see

Psalm LXXXIX

A Psalm of David
Happy is your face
on the fence
between the crown
and the prayer
better than the starving
words until the end
of the heavens of
the future

Psalm CVI

A Psalm of separation

Again
and again
the cloud
goes up
within it
what

rain
never
arrives

still

the mountains
grow
dividing
between night
and more night

Psalm CXXXVI

service of
the Temple

Psalm CXL

Thou shalt not sleep

Psalm CXLIX

The tetragrammaton-(God's unpronounceable name)

9 780738 823249